Six-Word Lessons

to Build Great Web Sites

100 Six-Word Lessons to Create Business Web Sites that Drive Your Brand and Grow Revenue

Mike Howell

Eric Peters

Six-Word Lessons to Build Great Web Sites

Six-Word Lessons to Build Great Web Sites
Editing by Patty Pacelli – pattypacelli.com

All rights reserved. No part of this book may be reproduced or transmitted in any form or by any means, electronic or mechanical including photocopying, recording or by any information storage or retrieval system, without the written permission of the publisher, except where permitted by law.

Copyright © 2010 by Eric Peters and Mike Howell

Published by Leading on the Edge International
704 228th Avenue NE #703
Sammamish WA 98074
leadingonedge.com

ISBN-10: 1-933750-24-3
ISBN-13: 978-1-933750-24-8

Six-Word Lessons to Build Great Web Sites

Legend has it that Ernest Hemingway was challenged by some friends to write a story in six words. Hemingway responded to the challenge with the following story: *For sale: baby shoes, never worn.*

The story tickles the imagination. Why were the shoes never worn? Were they too small? Did the baby die? Was the baby not able to wear shoes? Any of these are plausible explanations left up to the reader's imagination.

This style of writing has a number of aliases: postcard fiction, flash fiction, micro fiction, and sudden fiction. Lonnie Pacelli, the series creator, was introduced to this style of writing by a friend over a cup of coffee. He was entranced with the idea and started thinking about how this extreme brevity of writing could apply in today's micro-burst communication culture of text messages, tweets, and wall posts. Thus the inspiration for the **Six-Word Lessons** series.

In **Six-Word Lessons to Build Great Web Sites** you will find 100 short, practical tips and ideas to help you build and maintain high quality Web sites that deliver results. Rather than pore through pages and pages of content trying to search for what you need, **Six-Word Lessons to Build Great Web Sites** gives them to you quickly and easily.

Our hope is that you're able to use the ideas from **Six-Word Lessons to Build Great Web Sites** to build high impact Web sites that drive your brand and grow revenue. Tell us how it's impacted you at story@6wordlessons.com.

Six-Word Lessons to Build Great Web Sites

Six-Word Lessons to Build Great Web Sites

Table of Contents

It Starts with the Right Strategy................ 7

Branding-The Point of the Arrow................. 19

Successful Principles of Web Based Marketing ... 33

Search Engine Optimization-More For Free 45

Search Engines and Search Engine Marketing 57

E-Commerce: Making Money With Your Site......... 69

Content Management Systems-Keeping Things Fresh 81

Getting Attention-Social Media and Blogging 91

Performance Analytics to Know Your Results 105

Picking a Vendor to Get Started................ 113

Six-Word Lessons to Build Great Web Sites

Six-Word Lessons to Build Great Web Sites

It Starts with the Right Strategy

1

Why do we have Web sites?

So, how do we shift our thinking and get started with Return on Investment (ROI) on our Web site? First, set a goal. Many companies have never asked themselves: "Why do we have a Web site?" Other questions too rarely asked include: "Ideally, what types of visitors would we like to attract to our Web site" or (this one is very important) "What do we want them to do when they get there?"

What's your Web site's big picture?

We've all been there--trying to plan for a new Web site. ROI can sometimes take a back seat to something frivolous if you're not focused. It's easy to get distracted but online goal setting doesn't have to be hard. It's a matter of identifying your business objective and tying it to a strategy. New Web site ROI can be tracked to the penny, as long as you can tie your actions to your objectives.

Become your biggest and best fan

Tell everybody and anybody who will listen about your site and your business. This especially means online. Write about you, your business, news, and accomplishments. Don't be shy--it may not always be of great interest to everyone, but it also propagates the site, your keywords and your URL into cyberspace.

Write content with customers in mind

Keywords are increasingly important as businesses compete for customers, as well as search engine visibility. Keywords are your connection to customers. Write content with customers in mind, then go back and insert keywords and phrases into the text you think searchers will type into the search engine box. Customer optimization should come before search engine optimization. After all, search engines don't buy products, customers do.

Find your niche and exploit it

What do you offer your customers? We are not necessarily referring to the actual product, service or solution. Rather, what is it that you offer that your customers can't find elsewhere? In the online world, nearly every space is filled. Competition is fierce. Not only do you have to worry about direct competitors, you also face unconventional competition for space. It's becoming increasingly necessary for businesses to figure out their niche, then exploit it.

Keep your message and site simple

The Dalai Lama once said that simplicity is the key to happiness in the modern world. This philosophy can be adapted to Web and digital design. Simplicity lasts. It is necessary in order to properly convey an idea. It's said that a message is composed of 60 percent body language, 10 percent speech and 30 percent tone of voice. If this were true for Web design, we could say 60 percent design, 10 percent actual content and 30 percent writing style.

Use the power of local search

The end result of local search is exclusive visibility that directs clients to your physical address and Web site. You also gain credibility beyond traditional search results as consumers begin to recognize your company as a trusted resource in the virtual world. More than 30 percent of Internet users like to search with a town, city or local keyword. Increasing your visibility increases the possibility they will drive to your business location to buy from you.

Never redirect away from your site

You have worked plenty hard to get potential customers to your site. Keep them there! Articles, resources, and white papers are all credible links to support your product or business. Look for options that keep your customers put. Rewrite the article with full credit given, use the link as a pop-up window without a toolbar. You wouldn't tell a customer to go down the street for information--don't do the same thing on your site.

9

Always be building on your database

Most successful businesses have a large database of contacts, including current and past clients, prospects, and suppliers, which they keep up-to-date and fully utilize. This is why your contact list is a goldmine for your business. The number and variety of strategies you can utilize with it are limitless, as are the results you can achieve from it. Using your database well can generate leads for your business and increase your sales.

Know who your site is targeting

The best way to establish who your target market is and how to position yourself is by conducting research. Use polls or surveys of current or prospective clients to get a better understanding of your audience. Your relationships are invaluable resources when trying to figure out who that is. It's hard to take yourself out of the situation and look in from an outside perspective. Rely on your relationships to give you that outsider's perspective.

Six-Word Lessons to Build Great Web Sites

Six-Word Lessons to Build Great Web Sites

Branding - The Point of the Arrow

Long tail searches for more results

The "long tail" would be the hundreds of terms that derive from your competitive keywords. Here's an example. Let's say you sell HD TV's. You want to rank for the competitive keyword HD TV. However, you also want to rank for 42-inch Samsung HD TV, how to choose the best HD TV, reviews for Plasma HD TVs, etc. As you can see, the long tail keywords are simply more targeted search terms than your original keyword.

Keep your colors consistent and complementary

The use of a color scheme is essential when organizing a Web site. You want your site to look uniform, well planned, and well designed. The colors you choose can be balanced, harmonizing, contrasting, or complementary, depending on the goal of your site. Colors can have a psychological effect on viewers, so it is important to consider that when organizing your scheme.

Smart sites use spell check religiously

Here's some quick advice. If you're going to ask people to give you money, spell-check your site. Ask a friend to look over your site for typos just like you would with a resume. If your objective is to get someone to give you money, the effort is definitely worth it. Or there are a variety of programs that can spell-check your site documents. If you search for "spell check Web page," you can also find sites that offer spell-checking of live Web pages.

Keep font size consistent and friendly

On the Internet you will begin to see a pattern with regard to font styles and sizes. Generally, common fonts, Times New Roman, Arial or Courier, are used. Standard size varies from 10 to 12, although it could go as large as 14. It's easier on the eyes, and if an accent such as bolding were added, the text would still be easy to read. Remember, by limiting the number of styles and sizes, you will make your pages more visitor-friendly--and that means more sales for you!

Pay attention to your site layout

In Web design, one of the most important elements in providing a Web site that your customers will really spend time at is something known as "user experience." This is simply the study of what the user of a Web site goes through (or experiences) when they visit said site. There are a few things that every Web site must have in order to function as it is supposed to. These are the header, navigation, content, footer, and in some cases a sidebar.

Keep your animation and sound limited

Annoying is the optimal word. Animation and sound can only hurt and it rarely enhances a site. Opening a site to suddenly blaring music or noises will likely result in a quick shut down long before you can communicate your message. If it's required or inevitable at least give the visitor the choice to play instead of forcing it upon them first.

Nobody likes pop-ups on your site

Pop-up ads made more sense during the early era of the Internet. People were a lot less apt to navigate away from pop-ups, and were more naive to the Web. Now, they garner either sighs or giggles. Clicks won't be generated by flashing bright colors, and opening up a new window. It will certainly lead to the user going somewhere else, and never returning to your site.

18

Make it easy to find stuff

Think about what content you have and how it's organized. Put as few clicks between your visitor and your information as possible. This is so important I'll repeat it: Put as few clicks between your visitor and your information as possible. The more you force visitors to click around your site, the more likely they'll abandon it. Even if they don't leave they might get annoyed, or not view as much of your content--either of which is bad for you.

Optimize all your pictures and video

If a picture file is too large, the Web site will take longer to download, and your visitors may get frustrated. Optimizing a picture file reduces the file size and helps it load faster. Making the background of a GIF image transparent reduces pixel size and some Web sites offer services that will analyze your Web site and tell you which objects can be reduced. Also use pictures sparingly on your Web page--select the good ones and save the rest for another page.

20

Careful how you use exclamation points

They can be perfect when used thoughtfully. But overused, they make a business message sound and look silly. We do need ways to express our enthusiasm and excitement in writing. But words can do much of the work for us.

No new windows for internal links

Keep your site flowing within one browser window whenever possible. Users don't like to deal with dozens of opened tabs and some visitors tend to quickly become angry with the disabled back-button. Furthermore, some visitors may not even realize that a new window was opened and hit the back-button mercilessly--without any result. That's not user-friendly and it is not a good user experience to strive for.

Are your site links obviously clickable?

Hyperlinks should look like hyperlinks. Give them a distinct style, so they cannot be confused with any of the other text on the page. Definitely choose a unique color not used anywhere else on your page, and consider using the well-worn convention of the link underline when necessary.

Six-Word Lessons to Build Great Web Sites

Successful Principles of Web Based Marketing

Make competition tracking a regular activity

In business, you always need to know what your competitors are doing. To survive you must perform competitive intelligence activities and monitor the broader market. Tracking your competitors is the only way to make sure you are thwarting threats, taking advantage of opportunities, marketing effectively, and, ultimately, winning in the marketplace.

I always think above the fold

Newspapers are folded in half so the only part of the front page people see before they decide to buy is what comes above the fold. In a similar way, the first impression visitors have of a Web site is what shows up in their browser before scrolling. This window is the above-the-fold space. The more visitors see with prominent branding, the easier it is for them to remember a Web site. Make sure the business name, logo, and tag line are obvious the moment a page loads.

Show off your staff with profiles

One danger of Web based business is the lack of human interaction. Don't keep one of the key pieces of your business hidden behind the facade of your Web site. Emphasize your staff's strengths, talents and experience. Show professional pictures of them and talk about their accomplishments. Give your Web site and your business the human feel.

Tell your customers what to do

Tell your customers what to do. Give them step by step instructions. Take them by the hand and show them the way! If you don't, your competitor will and guess who will get their business. "Buy now!" for an e-commerce site, "Instant quote," "Check out our latest product special!" Determine where exactly you want your customers to go and why, then tell them to go there and do it!

Keep one Web page per topic

Focus. The key to success is to focus. Customers search for one item at a time and your site should reflect that tendency. No one searches for "French bread and bicycle repair" at the same time. Your site is likely about complementary products and services. Just parse out the topics that stand alone and write about them. These are called landing pages.

Site should never have broken links

They are sloppy, unprofessional, and frustrating for a user. Imagine the damage they can do for a search engine too. Use services to search your site and find every broken link and fix it. Nothing says lazy faster than telling somebody to check something out and nothing is there.

Navigation must be easy and intuitive

Don't underestimate the importance of a good navigational system. With the sheer quantity of multimedia and information sources available today, audiences are becoming increasingly impatient when it comes to locating information, especially on the Web. Web visitors are quick to pick up and move on if a Web site is not easy to navigate. In fact, reports show that thirty seconds of fruitless searching is all the average visitor will tolerate.

30

You must have calls to action

Ideally you want the most important call to action to be pretty obvious upon first scan. This means above the fold and centered on the page. It's true that it's okay to have longer pages these days that extend beyond the fold. People know how to scroll. It still makes sense to put your call to action where people won't miss it. Grab your visitor's attention with what little time you might have.

Make sure each page has value

Don't create pages simply to create pages. Think through the details and information you are writing about and give information that has value. Volume without value is just fluff. Fluff makes for a quick exit. Content of interest builds credibility and trust, keeping your customers coming back for more.

Put contact information on every page

Follow the principles of making actions easy for your customers--don't make them search for traditional ways of getting in contact with you. Phone numbers, e-mail addresses, or physical address if relevant should have prominent placement at the top and bottom of all the pages of your site.

Yes, teens look at sites differently

Teens like cool-looking graphics and they pay more attention to a Web site's visual appearance than adult users do. Still, the sites that teens rated the highest for subjective satisfaction were sites with a relatively modest, clean design. They typically marked down overly glitzy sites as too difficult to use. Teenagers like to do stuff on the Web, and dislike sites that are slow or that look fancy but behave clumsily.

Six-Word Lessons to Build Great Web Sites

Search Engine Optimization - More For Free

Don't build your site with Flash

Most important: not every search engine is able to crawl and index the content of Flash movies. Even those that can often do it with errors. This is especially true with a Web site fully implemented in Flash as a single file. Search engines just wouldn't be able to direct visitors to the proper page within that file.

Too many pictures is no good

If a picture tells a thousand words then what does one thousand pictures tell? Too much. Keep it simple and choose images that tell the story or emphasize the point, and write text that supports the picture. Less is more for the experience, loading speeds, and overall appearance.

The importance of proper key words

What do you think happens if you pick a bunch of words or phrases that people aren't actually searching for? Or you don't think of all the hundreds of other keywords that relate to your product or service and therefore lose potential clients? You might have the best of intentions when thinking of your own keywords, but it's better to do a thorough keyword search before beginning any Web site project.

URL, page title and H1 tags

The trifecta of good organic SEO ranking. If and when possible these three should match up with the key words or actual product or service. It can be the single most powerful tool to get ranked.

38

Use the power of free directories

Make the brilliance and dexterity of the Internet work for you. Use the power of free directories to post your information-rich articles and link them to your Web site through the reference section. Viewers will be sufficiently enticed to visit your page if you convey your message in a lucid and entertaining style while offering extensive knowledge.

Build inbound links from other sites

Perhaps the least understood step in the process, it's perhaps the place where you can have the most impact on your results. This involves making a concerted effort to build links to your site from other sites of relevance. Google views these links as "votes" for your site and increases your rankings. Organic listings will be greatly measured based not only on the number of inbound links but where are they from.

Include a menu on every page

While you should provide a way for users to get back to your home page quickly, you shouldn't force them to go home before they can go somewhere else. Include a menu on the left or the top of each page. Users clearly dislike links at the bottom of long pages. On long pages, you'll want navigation elements on BOTH the bottom and the top or left, so that users who have read a lengthy page don't have to scroll back up to get to the menus.

Create good landing pages for keywords

Do not send visitors to your home page and force them to search for what they are looking for! If you don't have a specific landing page created for your specific offer, create one! Build it with keyword rich text and the information users seek to make it the de facto authority on that subject.

Use descriptive link text for hyperlinks

You don't want to be ranked for "click here" or "read about it here." Google looks at a link, what it says, and then where it is going. Highlight keywords through out your site and link pages by hyperlinking those keywords to the appropriate landing pages. When Google indexes your site it will emphasize those words and rank the resulting landing page higher for that keyword.

Text is text, pictures are images

As with any Web page you want to optimize, there are certain things you can do to increase the ranking of the images on the Web page as well (and overall definition of the topic of your site as a whole). Use images to emphasize points and text on each page. Technically make sure that you use descriptive image names such as "blue wicker gift basket.jpeg" rather than "P103498229.jpg." And make sure to use the same description for the alt text of the image.

Six-Word Lessons to Build Great Web Sites

Six-Word Lessons to Build Great Web Sites

Search Engines and Search Engine Marketing

Search engines--how they do that?

The term is often used to describe both crawler-based sites and human-powered directories. Crawler-based search engines, such as Google, create their listings automatically. If you change your pages, they find them. A human-powered directory, such as the Open Directory, depends on humans. You submit a short description for your entire site, or editors write one for sites they review. A search looks for matches only in the descriptions submitted.

Pay for placement is a strategy

Pay per click search engines (PPC) has become an integrated part of search engine optimization. They are all based on the auction principle. You make a bid for a certain keyword or keyword phrase, and the amount decides the ranking. Google's Adwords program gives you access to the search engine result pages of Google. There are strategies where PPC makes sense over organic--whether it is particularly heavy competition or branding reasons.

When you search every word matters

Generally, all the words you put in the query will be used. It's at the very least something to keep in mind when developing pages or researching keywords. If your business subscribes to the "niche" philosophy then it's also important to match your pages and text to fulfill that niche. For example if you had an auto repair shop that focused on pre-1980 Italian sports cars - then make sure all of that information is included regularly throughout the site.

How will the written page look?

A search engine is not human, it's a program that matches the words you give to pages on the Web. Use words that are most likely to appear. For example, instead of "my head hurts," say "headache, because that's the term a medical page will use. The query, "in what country are bats considered good luck?" is clear, but the answer may not have those words. Instead, use, "bats are considered good luck in," because that is probably what the right page will say.

You should target Google's golden triangle

In a Google result page one point is immediately above the first organic listing, a second point is to the far right of that first result, third point is to the left, three listings down. That's the Google Golden Triangle. Want some stats? In tests, 100 percent of the users look at the first three results, and only 20 percent of the users will look at the tenth search result. Moreover, after being looked at, there is a fraction of a second to convince the user that clicking it will satisfy his query.

Visits starts with a simple search

Eighty-five percent of all Web activity starts with a search. It has been observed and proven by research that more and more businesses such as yours are seeing great results with online advertising. Millions of people search online each day for products, services and information. Google is the number one choice for all these searches.

Look for your site on Google

You never know where you might pop up, or who is talking about you. Find out by searching for yourself. Open a Google page and type in "site:www.yoursite.com" and hit enter. What comes up is everywhere Google has found your site. Check it out--hopefully it all good news, but it could also be a complaint, misreference, etc. Keep your image and your site clean!

Submit your site map to Google

A Sitemap is a list of the pages on your Web site. Submitting a Sitemap helps make sure the search engines know about all the pages on your site, including URLs that may not be discoverable by normal crawling processes.

Leverage the power of Webmaster Tools

Google Webmaster Tools is a free service that provides a wealth of information directly from Google. Once you have verified a site with Google, they will give you access to all sorts of information. Google Webmaster Tools will show all types of errors with a site, set site defaults, and analyze meta descriptions and title tags. They will discover top search queries, manage site links and enhance 404 error pages.

Analytics get you under the hood

Google offers tons of free tools to do all kinds of things like create online spreadsheets, find directions to a local restaurant, manage your photo collection, or share a family calendar. Whether you have an established Web presence or are looking to launch your first site, there is a free tool from Google you should be using. It's called called Google Analytics and it provides very detailed insight into how people are interacting with your Web site.

Six-Word Lessons to Build Great Web Sites

E-Commerce: Making Money With Your Site

Customers--bus drivers of the marketplace

More than ever, businesses need to listen closely to what customers are saying (which by the way, is evolving) and for an e-commerce site this is even more important. It is absolutely critical that an e-commerce site offers a friendly, easy to use, interactive, and responsive shopping experience. If not, users will find one that does.

Not fulfilling orders-- a death spiral

A great way to drive users away from your site it to take orders then not deliver. Build relationships with multiple vendors to ensure you have access to inventory. Work with reliable shippers and allow users to track their delivery. If you take an order, be able to deliver on your commitment.

Returning visitors versus first-time users

There is a difference between first-time visitors and repeat shoppers. Help your repeat shoppers by not showing them the same introductory instructions, messages, or questions they saw the first time they came to your site. This creates a better user experience and will help drive more repeat traffic.

Different users will have different styles

Consider in your content and calls to action that you will be dealing with a wide range of user styles. Some users search only on weekends, some during the evenings, some early in the week. Your calls to action and content should be tailored to each style. Useful information can be cutoff times for specials, shipping deadlines, and other similar calls to action.

Privacy policies and shopping cart abandonment

Shoppers are still sensitive about their privacy. Studies suggest you can lose up to half your shoppers by not clearly addressing concerns about privacy. Be sure your privacy policy is tailored to your business and not borrowed from someone else, that it's up to date and easy to find on your site. Being able to easily find your phone number on your site also helps build confidence.

Different users search in different areas

Users do not all think alike, nor do they search alike. In order for your products and services to reach the widest audience, make them available in different categories. Include suggestions for up-selling and cross-selling. For example, if you sell sporting goods, list items like baseball gloves, bats, batting stands, and other accessories together. Consider listing items according to price. You may up-sell to a more expensive item if they know it is available.

Keep it simple to spark interest

Make it as simple to buy as you possibly can. One reason users leave without buying is because some sites can be too hard to navigate. Information may be unclear or there are too many steps to complete a purchase. Make your phone number clear on your site. It creates peace of mind that helps drive conversion rates when questions arise.

Market sites to drive user traffic

Having a well designed e-commerce site is only part of the puzzle. You'll need to market it to draw attention. Build your database by offering specials to get visitors to register their e-mail addresses. A good database is essential to outbound marketing programs like newsletters and e-mail blasts. Keep up with your SEO efforts to rank as high as possible during keyword searches and consider other forms of advertising like magazines or trade shows to draw attention.

Build sales by making payment easy

Online shoppers need to give you money, over the Internet, when buying from your Web site. This has become much easier to do these days. You can set up an online merchant account or pick from a number of trustworthy online payment vendors, such as PayPal, which has become the largest vendor. Weigh the ease of getting started plus your up-front cost and compare to a possible longer term option with higher cost per transaction to decide which is best for your model.

/ Getting educated online--what a concept!

E-commerce is a very fast-paced space and things change quickly. With a little effort you can keep up with events and trends by reading from the vast amount of information available on the Internet. A few good sources to get started are Web Commerce Today (webcommercetoday.com) or E-Commerce Times (ecommercetimes.com).

Six-Word Lessons to Build Great Web Sites

Content Management Systems-- Keeping Things Fresh

Content management systems benefits: part one

There are several reasons frequent updates to your Web site are important. One reason is that a site updated with the right kind of content is simply more interesting to visit. It gives your users reason to visit your site more often, which will lead to them knowing more about your company, and that should lead to more transactions.

Content management systems benefits: part two

Before CMS tools, the group overseeing the success of a Web site, usually marketing, had to submit changes to the group that did the updates, usually IT. Problem was that IT had their own priorities. Today's CMS tools allow users with basic business computer skills to update complex content, in a timely manner, as easily as sending an e-mail or creating a word document.

Content management systems benefits: part three

Search engines look for the right type of content when crawling sites, but they also look at the frequency of your updates. That means frequently updating your site with the right type of content will help your site get crawled more often by search engines. More frequent search engine visits will help create higher ranking results, which will lead to an increase in visitors.

67

Choose a CMS that fits you

Typically a CMS allows for nontechnical users to update their Web sites. Look around and you'll see that some systems offer a varied range of features. Some are needed, but some are more complex and less intuitive than others. Be sure that a CMS you invest in meets your needs without offering too many features you won't use. These extra features work for some, but can mean extra complexity you that can reduce your ROI.

68

It's quality not quantity that counts

Know your customers, understand their habits and include only as much of the proper content as you need to tell your story. Be disciplined and careful to not overdo it. A good CMS offers tremendous flexibility compared to a static site, but don't fall so in love with your new capability that you get carried away building content or adding "things" to your site that don't add value just because they are easy to add.

69

Redesign? Time to clean your content

Like an electronic spring cleaning, clean up existing content when converting to a new content management system. Make time to get customer input and look at your Web analytics to see what content is the most important to your users. In all but a few cases, this is the time to reduce existing low value content. Studies suggest the average amount content available for deleting is in the range of 40 percent. This will help your Web site look and work better.

Why more can sometimes be less

When figuring CMS ROI, consider both expenses and savings. Yes there are typically upfront fees and sometimes ongoing costs, but be sure to consider things like the savings that come from not having to pay highly compensated programmers to make changes to your site once your CMS is implemented. Compare your upfront and other costs AND savings to determine your true ROI.

You won't please everyone every time

Like most change, there's a good chance some of your staff will resist moving to a CMS. Work flows will change for the people adding your content and job security may be a concern for staff developers. Keep these challenges in mind and be ready to manage the people side of this technical change to get the most ROI.

More about content-- less about design

A theory behind content management sytems is that once a design is set, the changes that really make a difference are in the content. By making content changes without worrying about impacting the design, the focus is only on content. This allows you to focus less on managing the technical impact of your changes and more on improving your messaging and cutting your time to delivery.

Getting Attention-- Social Media and Blogging

Isn't social media just a fad?

Is Facebook just something that keeps college students busy? Is Twitter for adults with too much time on their hands? The answer to both of these is NO! Social media tools offer amazing potential for businesses to spread their message, sometimes to an entirely new audience, and at a much lower cost. Like anything else, to be successful a little luck might help, but stay in control of your luck by planning well, working hard and being creative.

Activity sparks interest and creates visibility

The bottom line is you have to be active. You won't keep up any gains or positive impact if users visit your pages and don't see regular updates. There's not much excitement in seeing the same lines over and over again and pretty soon you'll lose momentum. Its easy to set up a Twitter account or Facebook page, but make sure you're ready to stay with to get maximum results.

Head in the sand: winning strategy?

In today's market, no matter what you say, you're not listening to your customers if you're not involved with Facebook, Twitter or any number of other tools. There could be tens, hundreds or even thousands of comments about your company going on that you're missing. Are they good? Are they bad? Do you know? Wouldn't you like to know? Do you think your boss would like you to know?

How to know what's getting said

It's actually very easy and doesn't take too much effort. Come up with a list of terms related to your company and enter them into one or more of the free online tools that track what is being written online. Addict-o-matic is a well known tool although there are many others to choose from.

Now that I know, what next?

Its really important to stay on top of what is said about you, since by definition, social media is not controlled. But how do you react to conversations and manage your reputation? In the most simple of terms, you just need to: 1. monitor and read what is being written 2. reward the positive 3. work to turn the negative into a positive. It's as easy as that!

Social media and old school marketing

Even with the growth in social media marketing, the statistics say this area should be used as an extension of generally accepted marketing methods. Don't replace other "old school" marketing activities with social media just yet, but look for areas where social media and existing marketing programs can work together. You'll most likely see better results overall and isn't that the goal?

Blogging--why bother? Define your goals

Like most other activities, it's useful to set goals for why you're blogging. Do you want to be seen as an expert within the industry? Is it to create awareness of your company? Is it just an outlet to have fun? Think about what you want to accomplish in 90 days, 6 months and 12 months, then build a "blogging plan" around these goals and schedules. Stay disicplined and measure your progress regularly.

Will video help my Web site?

Video is one of the fastest growing ways to personalize Web sites. Good video can be fun; it's very personal and can be highly informative. Be careful though, because it can also be incredibly boring and almost painful to watch. If done poorly, video can be a real turn-off. Make sure that your video elicits the intended positive response or leave it off your site.

Blogging--be yourself and be inviting

Readers come to your blog looking more for your opinions than to get industry news. You'll get more attention from blogging when you do it from your heart than if you blog from your business plan. Make every effort to ensure your personality shows through in the words you write.

Choose your voice and be consistent

Keep in mind that like the rest of your Web site, a corporate blog is part of your brand. It is good to ask yourself if you expect more attention from using a personal tone, a company tone, or some other "industry critic" tone. Whichever tone you choose, be consistent.

Build your database quickly by blogging

As an e-mail marketer you understand how difficult and important it is to build subscriber lists. Blogging can be a big help with this. By providing educational information or thought provoking opinions and inviting readers to subscribe, you can build your data base without being intrusive.

Getting fresh links to drive SEO

Social media is a great source for listing inbound links which can help improve your SEO and there are a number of things you can do to grow these. For one, keep putting out content that has staying power. Link to old content on your site when appropriate. Promote the sharing of your content. Include buttons to make it easy for people to share your content on their social networks of choice.

Six-Word Lessons to Build Great Web Sites

Six-Word Lessons to Build Great Web Sites

Performance Analytics to Know Your Results

Traffic quality check--optimized or not?

Traffic quality is critical to success--attracting the wrong audience for several months, or only getting a small portion of the right audience can have a long lasting impact on online marketing ROI. For SEO campaigns, be sure to put in the effort to refine targeting (negative keywords, site/vertical, geo-targeting, etc.) and continually monitor how well this targeting is working. Don't let too much time pass when a change might have been in order.

Which is right--free or paid?

There are a number of tools available online with Google Analytics being one of the best known. Most any of the tools will allow you to track which keywords are sending you traffic from where, and which words are the most and least profitable. Be prepared to find that there are limitations with the free tools, as many vendors prefer you to upgrade to fee-based options before you get a robust set to analytic capability.

Keep peeling the analytical onion layers

What do the numbers really say? What products are doing well? Which geographic areas are buying what? What time of the day or week are most users making their purchases? Are there demographics you should investigate for more opportunity? Why are bounce rates decreasing? Be sure you have metrics that can be measured against so you can see trends and take action.

Answers are more in the trends

Interestingly, different vendors will not always offer the same Web site analytics results because they use different algorithims to get their information. No matter which tool you use, the real value is not really in the specific data, but more in the trends. If you see a trend that shows certain products increasing when entering a weekend, you can add specials or some other tactic to sell during the slower early weekday time frame.

Analyze your overall mix for clarity

Remember it's possible that other marketing activity can impact your hit rates and skew your Web site analytics. Word of mouth, a separate magazine or TV campaign, or some other variable might spike your traffic. Be sure to compare traffic sources and compare them by month over month and alongside other campaigns to make sure you know what really caused a change in activity.

൯൦

Track user habits for meaningful insights

Everyone is familiar with the recorded "this call may be monitored for training purposes" message. The same technology is available for Web sites and you can follow exactly what users are doing on your site. You can record their actual activity and see specifically where they go, how much time they spend on which pages, and where they bounce from your site. This allows you to study why users leave your site prior to completing a transaction and work on a solution.

Track and measure only one area

There are many areas of your Web site that affect the user experience. One useful analytic strategy is to pinpoint a specific area and isolate it. Measure, compare and adjust as needed. In other words, don't try to change six areas at once and look for results, because you might see a change, but you may not know what really caused it.

Picking a Vendor to Get Started

Sounds too good to be true

Everyone has received e-mail SPAM "guaranteeing #1 Google ranking," or some other "promise the moon" type of offer. Any vendor that promises or guarantees search engine success, #1 Google rankings or anything of the kind should be avoided. There's just no such thing as a guarantee. Don't fall for this no matter how much you're inclined to.

How long until I see results?

Sometimes search engine results can happen within weeks, but this is not the norm. More likely it may take sixty to ninety days before a solid SEO effort really starts to get traction. Part of it depends on how many of your competitors are trying to do the same thing, how well their strategies are working, and how long they have been after it. Be aggressive but be realistic.

Open source programming pros and cons

There are a large number of free open source programming tools that many Web site firms use to build their "platforms." Sometimes they are cheaper, but the tradeoff is they tend to come in modular blocks that limit your choice for the look and flow of your site. They can also limit your ability to drive SEO.

Browser beware: make sure you work

Make sure your vendor's platform works on the many browsers in use today. Consider that less that 50 percent of us use Internet Explorer, with the rest split between Firefox, Safari, Opera, and others. You don't want to leave anyone out, so verify that the Web site platform you choose is compatible with all browsers, and test regularly to be sure browser updates don't impact you in a negative way.

Are you ready for mobile devices?

Make sure your potential vendor solution is mobile device ready. A rapidly growing part of the user base is using mobile phones more and more. These devices and others with smaller screens have different requirements. Make sure your new site will meet the needs of this huge and important audience.

Advantages and disadvantages of outsourced hosting

By spreading the costs of servers, backup, maintenance, and support people over a number of users, hosted platforms may be less expensive than keeping things in house. Upgrades in a hosted model tend to be free or at least cheaper than a licensed model. Licensed models tend to not come with upgrades unless you have an ongoing service agreement of some type.

Existing portfolios paint very clear pictures

An important step in your Web site partner vetting process should be to check their existing portfolios. Past performance is a great indication of what they'll deliver in the future. Make sure you like what they've done for others. If you don't, it's likely you won't like the one they do for you.

White hat good, black hat bad

Not all SEO techniques are the same, and in fact, some actually conflict with search engine "terms of service." Known in the industry as "black hat" techniques, these include hidden text and keyword stuffing among others. Approved SEO techniques are known as "white hat" and reputable firms stick to white hat approaches. Keep an eye out for techniques that sound like black hat in style. These can actually backfire and get your site blacklisted.

100

Go with your gut when choosing

After all of your analytical check boxes are marked, make sure the vendor you're about to choose is someone you can work with. You're ready to start a partnership that will last years. Ask yourself the following: Do we get along on a personal level? Can we work closely? When everything else is equal, ask your gut and lean toward the vendor that "feels" right.

See the entire Six-Word Lesson Series at *6wordlessons.com*

Go to efellemedia.com to learn how efelle media can build a great Web site for you

Proof

Made in the USA
Charleston, SC
26 May 2010